CHOUX

CHOUX

Chic & delicious French pastries

Hannah Miles

photography by Kate Whitaker

RYLAND PETERS & SMALL
LONDON • NEW YORK

Senior Designer Megan Smith
Commissioning Editor
Stephanie Milner
Production Meskerem Berhane
Art Director Leslie Harrington
Editorial Director Julia Charles

Prop Stylist Jo Harris
Food Stylist Lucy McKelvie
Indexer Hilary Bird

Author's acknowledgements
With heartfelt thanks to all at RPS for their beautiful work on this book and to Kate Whitaker for stunning photography. Thanks also to Jo and Lucy for the wonderful styling. Much love to Heather and the Girls at HHB agency and to my friends, family and colleagues at MCL, SFP, Amphenol and Irvin's Teas who ate all the choux buns along the way.

Dedication
To Justina, Sheelah and Damian, with love xx

First published in 2014
by Ryland Peters & Small
20–21 Jockey's Fields,
London WC1R 4BW
and
519 Broadway, 5th Floor,
New York NY 10012
www.rylandpeters.com

10 9 8 7 6 5 4 3 2 1

Text © Hannah Miles 2014
Design and photographs © Ryland Peters & Small 2014

ISBN: 978-1-84975-495-8

Printed and bound in China

A CIP record for this book is available from the British Library.

Note There are certain health risks associated with whipped cream so always practice food safety by using fresh cream before it's expiry date and storing filled choux buns in an airtight container in the refrigerator until ready to serve.

CONTENTS

INTRODUCTION

Choux – a buttery pastry which is as light as a feather – makes the most amazing desserts and cakes I know.

Choux pastry is one of the best store cupboard standbys as the main ingredients you need are flour, butter and eggs. In about half an hour you can have delicate pastries to serve which can be filled with whipped cream or other fillings of your choosing. If you don't have any filling available then why not try the delicate *Choquettes* on page 23, simply topped with sugar nibs or chocolate chips. They are utterly moreish, particularly straight from the oven.

Initially the process for making choux pastry can seem tricky. I have to confess, that when I was learning to bake, for a long time choux pastry was my nemesis and on a few occasions it has reduced me to tears. That said, once you have mastered the knack of choux pastry, it is very easy to prepare and can produce amazing desserts very quickly. You just need a good understanding of the texture of the pastry and to follow the steps on pages 8–9 carefully.

Once you have prepared your choux pastry it can be piped into a wide variety of shapes. Classic éclairs are oblong choux buns which are often topped with icing. These are traditionally filled with either whipped cream or *crème patissière* which can be piped in through a small hole in the éclair or you can cut the éclair in half and sandwich it together with cream. Profiteroles are small balls of choux pastry that are generally filled with whipped cream and served with a sauce to pour over. I don't know anyone who can resist a chocolate profiterole! Choux buns are larger and often served topped with glacé icing. They are generally cut in half and filled with a wide variety of fillings. *Paris Brest* (named after the Paris to Brest cycle ride) are rings of choux pastry in the shape of a bicycle wheel. They can be piped either using a round nozzle or with a star nozzle which gives the rings a pretty, fluted effect when baked. *Religieuse* are another popular type of choux dessert with a choux ring topped with a small ball of choux pastry, said to resemble nuns. Choux pastry is really very versatile and can be formed into almost any shape you wish using a piping bag and nozzles, such as the choux hearts on page 50. I find that disposable icing bags are really useful for making choux pastry as most of the recipes in this book call for two or three piping bags.

This book contains all the classic choux recipes such as chocolate profiteroles with rich chocolate sauce and *Paris Brest*, filled with hazelnut praline and chocolate and vanilla éclairs. The Fruity chapter has a wide variety of fruit-filled choux pastries, from amaretto and peach *Paris Brest* to blackcurrant éclairs. For more unusual, dainty recipes the Fancy chapter contains Earl Grey tea buns with delicate tea-flavoured custard, rose and raspberry choux and violet éclairs. Finally, in the Dessert chapter, choux pastry is used to make a variety of spectacular party treats such as *Gâteau St Honoré* on page 63 and an amazing *croquembouche* on page 60. These recipes take some time to prepare but are definitely worth the effort. Whatever flavour combination you prefer, there are recipes in this book that all will enjoy.

BASIC CHOUX PASTRY

This basic choux recipe is used throughout the book. It needs a good strong arm and I find it is better beaten by hand than in a mixer as it is important to feel when the dough it ready.

Unlike shortcrust and puff pastry, choux has a high moisture content as it contains water and lots of eggs. It is this moisture which causes the sticky choux paste to puff up into delicate pastry shells. It is important to weigh your ingredients accurately and to sift as much air into the flour for best results. The pastry can be made with water alone or a combination of water and milk, which gives a richer flavour.

Single quantity
65 g plain flour
50 g butter, cut into cubes
75 ml milk and 75 ml water
    or 150 ml water
1 teaspoon caster sugar
a pinch of salt
2 large eggs

Some of the recipes in this book call for more than one quantity of pastry. Make in batches of no more than two quantities.

1 Sift the flour onto a sheet of baking parchment twice to remove any lumps and to add as much air as possible. **(A)**

2 Heat the butter in a saucepan with the milk and water (or just water if preferred), sugar and salt until the butter is melted. As soon

A   B   C

D

E

F

as the butter is melted remove the pan from the heat and quickly shoot the sifted flour in all in one go. It is important not to let the water heat for longer than it takes to melt the butter as this will evaporate some of the water and so there will be less liquid for the pastry. **(B)**

3 Beat the mixture very hard with a wooden spoon or whisk until the dough forms a ball and no longer sticks to the sides of the pan and the pan is clean. At first the mixture will seem very wet but don't worry as it will come together after few minutes once the flour absorbs the water. It is important to really beat the mixture well at this stage. Leave to cool for about five minutes. **(C)**

4 Whisk the eggs in a separate bowl and then beat a small amount at a time into the pastry using a wooden spoon or a balloon whisk. The mixture will form a sticky paste which holds its shape when you lift the whisk up. When you first add the eggs and begin beating the mixture will split slightly. This is normal and the pastry will come back together as you continue to beat. The mixture must be beaten hard at each stage. **(D) (E)**

5 If the mixture is runny and does not hold its shape, unfortunately it cannot be used as it will not rise. Adding more flour to the mixture will not work. If this happens I tend to start again, although I have read that you can make a second batch of choux pastry and add this wet mixture in, in place of the eggs and it will be rescued. **(F)**

Use the pastry following the steps in each recipe.

CRÈME PÂTISSIÈRE

Single quantity
1 egg and 1 egg yolk
1 heaped tablespoon cornflour
60 g caster sugar
150 ml double cream
100 ml milk

Whisk the egg and egg yolk with the cornflour and sugar until very thick and pale yellow in colour. Place the cream and the milk in a saucepan and bring to the boil. Pour over the egg mixture, whisking all the time. Return to the pan and whisk over a gentle heat until the mixture becomes very thick. Pour into a bowl and leave to cool. Chill in the refrigerator until needed.

CLASSIC

Chocolate éclairs, delicate pastries with vanilla filling, and topped
with a rich chocolate ganache, are the most popular of choux pastries.

CLASSIC CHOCOLATE ÉCLAIRS
with crème pâtissière

1 quantity Basic Choux
   Pastry (see page 8)

For the filling
Single quantity *crème
   pâtissière* (see page 9)
1 teaspoon vanilla bean
   paste
100 ml double cream

For the chocolate ganache
200 g plain chocolate
100 ml double cream
30 g butter
1 tablespoon golden syrup
   or light corn syrup

*a baking tray lined with
   baking parchment
   or a silicon mat
2 piping bags fitted with
   large round nozzles
12 paper cases, to serve*

Makes 12

Preheat the oven to 200°C (400°F) Gas 6. Spoon the choux pastry into the piping
bag and pipe 12 lengths of pastry, about 10 cm long, onto the baking tray,
a small distance apart. Pat down any peaks in the pastry using a clean wet finger.
Sprinkle a little water into the bottom of the oven to create steam which will help
the choux pastry to rise. Bake in the oven for 10 minutes, then reduce the oven
temperature to 180°C (350°F) Gas 4 and bake for a further 15–20 minutes until
the pastry is crisp. Remove from the oven and using a sharp knife cut a small
slit into each éclair to allow any steam to escape. Leave to cool.

Prepare the *crème pâtissière* for the filling following the
method on page 9, adding the vanilla paste with the milk.

For the chocolate ganache topping, heat
all the ingredients in a bowl over a pan
of simmering water until melted. Dunk
the top of each éclair into the ganache,
then leave to set on a cooling rack.

When ready to serve, whisk
the double cream to stiff peaks
and fold into the *crème pâtissière*.
Spoon into a piping bag. Make
a small hole in each éclair
using a sharp knife and
pipe until full.

Serve straight
away or store in the
refrigerator for up
to two days.

These are a chocoholic's delight. Munching through the cocoa choux pastry, chocolate ganache, white chocolate drizzle and chocolate curls prompted our village sewing circle to name them "Death by Chocolate"!

TRIPLE CHOCOLATE CHOUX BUNS

1 quantity Basic Choux
   Pastry (see page 8 but
   follow method here)
10 g cocoa powder

For the chocolate glaze
200 g dark chocolate
100 ml double cream
30 g butter
1 tablespoon golden syrup

To decorate
50 g white chocolate, melted
chocolate curls

For the filling
300 ml whipping cream

2 piping bags fitted with
   round nozzles
2 large baking trays lined
   with baking parchment

Makes 14

Preheat the oven to 200°C (400°F) Gas 6.

Make the choux pastry as instructed on page 8, adding the cocoa powder to the flour before sifting.

Spoon the chocolate choux pastry into a piping bag and pipe 14 balls onto the prepared baking trays, a small distance apart. Using a clean, wet finger, smooth down any peaks. Sprinkle a little water into the bottom of the oven to create steam which will help the choux pastry to rise. Bake each tray in the oven for 10 minutes, then reduce the oven temperature to 180°C (350°F) Gas 4 and bake for a further 15–20 minutes until the pastry is crisp. Remove from the oven and cut a slit into each bun to allow the steam to escape. Allow to cool then make a small hole in the base of each bun ready for piping the filling in later.

For the chocolate glaze, put the chocolate, cream, butter and syrup in a heatproof bowl set over a pan of simmering water and simmer until the chocolate has melted and the sauce is smooth and glossy. Reserve a large tablespoon of the chocolate glaze for the filling and let it cool. While still warm, dip the buns into the remaining glaze and place onto a cooling rack. To decorate, dip a fork into the melted white chocolate and drizzle thin lines of it over the buns. Sprinkle with chocolate curls and allow to set.

When you are ready to serve, place the reserved and cooled chocolate glaze with the whipping cream in a bowl and whisk to stiff peaks. Spoon into a piping bag and pipe into each of the buns, through the hole in the base. Serve immediately or store in the refrigerator for up to two days.

VANILLA ÉCLAIRS
with Chantilly cream

1 quantity Basic Choux
    Pastry (see page 8)

For the icing & decoration
150 g fondant icing
    sugar, sifted
1 teaspoon vanilla extract
food colouring (optional)
sugar flowers
100 g caster sugar

For the Chantilly cream
½ vanilla pod
1 tablespoon fondant icing
    sugar, sifted
350 ml double cream

*a large baking tray, lined
  with baking parchment
  or a silicon mat,
2 piping bags fitted with
  round nozzles*

Makes 12

With origins in nineteenth-century France, the éclair remains one of the most popular pastries today. This version is filled with a classic Chantilly cream, a sweetened cream with vanilla seeds.

Preheat the oven to 200°C (400°F) Gas 6. Spoon the choux pastry into a piping bag and pipe 12 lengths of pastry, about 10 cm long onto the baking tray, a small distance apart. Pat down any peaks in the pastry using a clean wet finger. Sprinkle a little water into the bottom of the oven to create steam which will help the choux pastry to rise. Bake in the oven for 10 minutes, then reduce the oven temperature to 180°C (350°F) Gas 4 and bake for a further 15–20 minutes until the pastry is crisp. Remove from the oven and using a sharp knife cut a small slit into each éclair to allow any steam to escape. Leave to cool.

For the icing, mix together the icing sugar, vanilla extract and 1–2 tablespoons of water until you have a smooth thick icing. Add 1–2 drops of food colouring of your choice, if desired, and mix. Spread the icing over the top of each éclair and decorate with sugar flowers. Leave to set.

For the Chantilly cream, split the vanilla pod in half with a sharp knife and carefully remove the seeds with the back of a knife. Place the seeds, icing sugar and double cream in a mixing bowl and whisk to stiff peaks. Place into the second piping bag. Make a small hole in the underside of each éclair using a sharp knife and pipe cream into each until they are full.

To make the spun sugar, heat the caster sugar in a heavy based saucepan. Do not stir the sugar but swirl the pan to prevent the sugar from burning. The sugar will start to caramelize but you need to watch it carefully at this stage as it can very quickly turn dark and burn. Remove from the heat once melted to a golden coloured caramel. Dip a fork into the sugar and pull it away from the pan to make long fine caramel strands. Immediately wrap each strand around a greased rolling pin to make sugar spirals. Serve immediately or store in the refrigerator for up to two days. The sugar work will become sticky over time so it is best to make the spirals just before serving.

This delicacy of choux pastry rings filled with praline cream was created in 1891 to celebrate the Paris to Brest cycle ride. Its classic shape was said to represent the wheels of the bicycles.

PARIS BREST

1 quantity Basic Choux
    Pastry (see page 8)
20 g hazelnuts, roasted,
    skinned and chopped

For the praline
100 g caster sugar
80 g hazelnuts, roasted,
    skinned and chopped

For the filling
300 ml double cream
1 tablespoon hazelnut butter
icing sugar, for dusting

2 large baking trays lined
    with baking parchment
    or a silicon mat
2 piping bags, one fitted
    with a round nozzle and
    one with a large star nozzle

Makes 9

Preheat the oven to 200°C (400°F) Gas 6. Spoon the choux pastry into one of the piping bags and pipe 9 rings about 7 cm in diameter onto the baking trays, a small distance apart. Pat down any peaks in the pastry using a clean wet finger. Sprinkle the pastry with the hazelnuts. Sprinkle a little water into the bottom of the oven to create steam which will help the choux pastry to rise. Bake in the oven for 10 minutes, then reduce the oven temperature to 180°C (350°F) Gas 4 and bake for a further 15–20 minutes until the pastry is crisp. Remove from the oven and cut a slit into each ring to allow any steam to escape. Leave to cool.

For the praline, heat the sugar in a saucepan until melted and golden brown. Do not stir the pan as the sugar is cooking but swirl it to ensure that the sugar does not burn. Spread the hazelnuts out on a greased baking tray or silicon mat and carefully pour over the melted sugar. Leave to cool and then blitz in a blender to very fine crumbs.

For the filling, whisk together the cream and hazelnut butter in a mixing bowl to stiff peaks. Stir through the praline – or, if you do not have time to make the praline, substitute an extra tablespoon of hazelnut butter – with a spatula, reserving a little powder to sprinkle over the top of the rings.

Spoon the cream into the second piping bag fitted with the star nozzle. Carefully, cut each ring in half horizontally with a sharp knife. Pipe a swirl of cream into the bottom of each bun. Top each with the hazelnut covered rings and then dust with icing sugar, sprinkle with a little of the praline powder and serve immediately. These are best eaten on the day they are made, but can be eaten the following day if stored in the refrigerator.

CHOCOLATE PROFITEROLES

1 quantity Basic Choux
Pastry (see page 8)
300 ml double cream,
whipped to stiff peaks

To serve with classic
chocolate sauce
160 g dark chocolate
(70% cocoa solids)
60 g butter
4 tablespoons double cream
3 tablespoons golden syrup

To serve with fondue
250 g plain chocolate
100 g white chocolate
80 ml almond liqueur
or other liqueur of your
choosing (coffee liqueurs
work well)
150 ml double cream

2 baking trays lined with
baking parchment
2 piping bags fitted with
round nozzles
a fondue pot (optional)

Makes 25

Chocolate profiteroles are one of the most popular desserts. This recipe has two different sauces to choose from – a classic chocolate pouring sauce or a warm chocolate fondue to dip the profiteroles into.

Preheat the oven to 200°C (400°F) Gas 6.

Spoon the choux pastry into one of the piping bags and pipe 25 small balls of pastry onto the baking trays, a small distance apart. Pat down any peaks in the pastry using a clean wet finger. Sprinkle a little water into the bottom of the oven to create steam which will help the choux pastry to rise. Bake in the oven for 10 minutes, then reduce the oven temperature to 180°C (350°F) Gas 4 and bake for a further 15–20 minutes until the pastry is crisp. Remove from the oven and cut a small slit into each ball to allow any steam to escape. Leave to cool.

When cool, spoon the whipped cream into a piping bag. Make a small hole in the base of each profiterole using a sharp knife and pipe cream in until each ball is full. Store in the refrigerator until you are ready to serve.

If serving the profiteroles with classic chocolate sauce, heat the chocolate, butter, cream and syrup in a saucepan until the chocolate has melted and the sauce is smooth and glossy. Pour the warm sauce over the profiteroles to serve.

If serving the profiteroles with fondue, place the plain and white chocolate in a heatproof bowl set over a pan of simmering water and add the almond liqueur and cream. Stir until the chocolate has melted and you have a thick chocolate sauce. Serve the sauce warm in a fondue pot with fondue sticks for the profiteroles so that you can dunk them into the sauce.

The profiteroles are best eaten on the day they are made, although can be eaten the following day if stored in the refrigerator.

These tiny choux buns are light and simple and although they contain no filling, with their crunchy sugar topping, they make a great mid morning snack. It is best to make these buns with a milk choux as they are richer in flavour but you can replace the milk with water if you prefer. Sugar nibs are available from online baking stores. They have more sugar in than regular choux pastry to improve the flavour and are also scented with vanilla.

CHOQUETTES

65 g plain flour
50 g unsalted butter,
    cut into cubes
75 ml water
75 ml milk
1 tablespoon caster sugar
1 tablespoon vanilla bean
    paste
a pinch of salt
2 eggs
sugar nibs for sprinkling
plain chocolate chips
    (optional)

a piping bag fitted with
    a round nozzle
2 large baking trays lined
    with baking parchment
    or a silicon mat

Makes 45

Sift the flour twice to remove any lumps. Heat the butter in a saucepan with the water, milk, sugar, vanilla bean paste and salt until the butter is melted. Bring to the boil, then quickly add the sifted flour all in one go and remove from the heat.

Beat hard with a wooden spoon or whisk until the dough forms a ball and no longer sticks to the sides of the pan. Leave to cool for about 5 minutes. Whisk the eggs and then beat into the pastry a small amount at a time using a wooden spoon or whisk. The mixture will form a sticky paste which holds its shape when you lift the whisk up.

Preheat the oven to 200°C (400°F) Gas 6,

Spoon the choux pastry into the piping bag and pipe 45 small balls of pastry a small distance apart on the trays. Using a wet finger smooth down any peaks. Top the pastry with sugar nibs. Sprinkle a little water into the bottom of the oven to create steam which will help the choux pastry to rise.

Bake each tray in the oven for 10 minutes, then reduce the oven temperature to 180°C (350°F) Gas 4 and bake for a further 10–15 minutes until the pastry is crisp.

Remove from the oven and cut a small slit in each bun straight away to allow any steam to escape. Sprinkle a few chocolate chips over the warm buns, if desired. They will melt onto the pastry slightly for added indulgence. Serve the buns warm or cold. The choquettes are best eaten on the day they are made but can be eaten the following day if stored in an airtight container.

These mini éclairs filled with coconut cream and topped with toasted coconut taste delicious. If you want to make them even more tropical you can add small pieces of pineapple to the éclair filling and add a little pineapple juice to the icing as well.

MINI COCONUT ÉCLAIRS

1 quantity Basic Choux
  Pastry (see page 8)

For the filling
300 ml double cream
1 tablespoon coconut cream
**1 tablespoon icing sugar,
  sifted**
**1 tablespoon Malibu
  or other coconut liqueur**

For the topping & icing
20 g coconut flakes
180 g icing sugar, sifted
1 tablespoon coconut cream

2 baking trays lined with
  baking parchment
  or a silicon mat
2 piping bags fitted with
  round nozzles

Makes 24

Preheat the oven to 200°C (400°F) Gas 6.

Spoon the choux pastry into one of the piping bags and pipe 24 lengths of pastry, about 4 cm long onto the baking trays, a small distance apart. Pat down any peaks in the pastry using a clean wet finger. Sprinkle a little water into the bottom of the oven to create steam which will help the choux pastry to rise.

Bake each tray in the oven for 10 minutes, reduce the oven temperature to 180°C (350°F) Gas 4 and bake for a further 15–20 minutes until the pastry is crisp. Remove from the oven and using a sharp knife cut a small slit into the sides of the éclairs to allow any steam to escape. Leave to cool. Make a hole in the base of each éclair ready for piping the filling in later.

For the filling, place the cream, coconut cream, icing sugar and Malibu in a bowl and whisk to stiff peaks. Spoon the cream into the other piping bag and pipe into each éclair through the holes you have made in the base. Store in the refrigerator until ready to serve.

Toast the coconut for the topping in a dry frying pan until it starts to turn golden brown, stirring all the time. Watch carefully as it can burn very easily. Tip into a bowl and leave to cool.

For the icing, mix together the icing sugar, coconut cream and a little water until you have a thick icing. Spread the icing over the éclairs and sprinkle with the coconut. Serve as soon as the icing has set or store in the refrigerator until needed. The éclairs are best eaten on the day they are made, although can be eaten the following day if you wish.

FRUITY

Blackcurrants always remind me of my Welsh grandparents as my Grandpa would grow them in abundance in his garden and my Gran would then use them to make the most delicious blackcurrant tarts. Both were excellent bakers and I am sure I inherited my love of baking from them. These blackcurrant éclairs are filled with juicy berries and have tangy blackcurrant icing on top.

BLACKCURRANT ÉCLAIRS

1 quantity Basic Choux
  Pastry (see page 8)

For the icing
180 g fondant icing
  sugar, sifted
1–2 tablespoons blackcurrant
  preserving syrup (see below)
50 g plain chocolate, melted

For the filling
350 ml double cream
290 g blackcurrants
  preserved in light syrup,
  drained but syrup reserved

a large baking tray, lined
  with baking parchment
  or a silicon mat
2 piping bags, one fitted with
  a large round nozzle and
  one with a star nozzle
12 paper cases, to serve

Makes 12

Preheat the oven to 200°C (400°F) Gas 6.

Spoon the choux pastry into the piping bag fitted with one of the round nozzles and pipe 12 lengths of pastry, about 10 cm long onto the baking tray, a small distance apart. Pat down any peaks in the pastry using a clean wet finger. Sprinkle a little water into the bottom of the oven to create steam which will help the choux pastry to rise.

Bake in the oven for 10 minutes, then reduce the oven temperature to 180°C (350°F) Gas 4 and bake for a further 15–20 minutes until the pastry is crisp. Remove from the oven and cut a small slit into each éclair with a sharp knife to allow any steam to escape. Leave to cool.

For the icing, whisk together the icing sugar with the blackcurrant syrup until you have a smooth, thick icing. Spread over the top of the éclairs. Drizzle the melted chocolate over the éclairs in thin lines using a fork, then leave the icing to set.

When you are ready to serve, whisk the double cream and 3 tablespoons of the blackcurrant syrup to stiff peaks. Spoon into the piping bag fitted with the star nozzle. Carefully cut each éclair in half lengthways and pipe a swirled line of the cream into the bottom of each éclair. Place some of the blackcurrants on top of the cream in each éclair. Cover with the iced tops and serve straight away or store in the refrigerator until needed. The éclairs are best eaten on the day they are made, although can be eaten the following day if you wish.

These éclairs are inspired by the elegant fresh fruit tarts that line the windows in French pâtisseries. They are simple to prepare and make a stunning addition to an afternoon tea cake stand.

FRESH FRUIT ÉCLAIRS

1 quantity Basic Choux Pastry (see page 8)

For the filling
300 ml double cream, whipped to stiff peaks

For the topping
150 g white chocolate
small pieces of fresh fruit of your choice (mango, grapes, raspberries and blueberries all work well)

2 piping bags fitted with round nozzles
a large baking tray lined with baking parchment or a silicon mat

Makes 12

Preheat the oven to 200°C (400°F) Gas 6. Spoon the choux pastry into one of the piping bags and pipe 12 lengths of pastry, about 10 cm in length onto the baking tray, a small distance apart. Pat down any peaks in the pastry using a clean wet finger. Sprinkle a little water into the bottom of the oven to create steam which will help the choux pastry to rise. Bake in the oven for 10 minutes, then reduce the oven temperature to 180°C (350°F) Gas 4 and bake for a further 15–20 minutes until the pastry is crisp. Remove from the oven and cut a small slit into each éclair to allow any steam to escape. Leave to cool.

Working in a cool place as the éclairs need to be filled with the cream before being decorated as the decoration is fragile, make a small hole in the base of each éclair and pipe until full of cream.

For the topping, place the white chocolate in a bowl over a saucepan of water and simmer until the chocolate is melted. Leave for about 10 minutes so that the chocolate cools slightly and thickens. Using a knife, spread some white chocolate neatly over the top of each éclair. Place the small pieces fruit in decorative patterns on top of the chocolate. It is important to only use small pieces otherwise they will be too heavy and cause the éclairs to topple over. It is best to do this with the éclairs balanced in the grooves of a cooling rack.

Serve the éclairs straight away or store in the refrigerator until needed. The éclairs are best eaten on the day they are made, although can be eaten the following day if stored in the refrigerator.

These choux rings are topped with an almond crumble which gives a great crunchy texture to the choux. If you are serving to children simply omit the alcohol.

PEACHES & CREAM CHOUX RINGS
with Amaretti crumble topping

2 quantity Basic Choux Pastry (see page 8)

For the crumble topping
70 g ratafia or amaretti biscuits
50 g golden marzipan
50 g butter, melted

For the filling
600 ml double cream
50 ml Amaretto or other almond liqueur
6 ripe peaches or nectarines
icing sugar, for dusting

2 baking trays lined with baking parchment or a silicon mat
2 piping bags fitted with large star nozzles

Makes 18

Begin by making the crumble topping. Break the ratafia biscuits to very small pieces using your hands. Finely chop the marzipan and add with the warm melted butter to the ratafia. Crush the mixture together with your hands until you have large crumbs of the mixture.

Preheat the oven to 200°C (400°F) Gas 6.

Spoon the choux pastry into a piping bag and pipe 18 rings about 7 cm in diameter onto the baking trays, a small distance apart. Pat down any peaks in the pastry using a clean wet finger. Top each ring with a little of the crumble topping. Do not worry if any of the crumbs fall onto the tray as these can be discarded after baking. Sprinkle a little water into the bottom of the oven to create steam which will help the choux pastry to rise.

Bake each tray in the oven for 10 minutes, then reduce the oven temperature to 180°C (350°F) Gas 4 and bake for a further 15–20 minutes until the pastry is crisp. Watch that the crumble topping does not burn towards the end of cooking. Remove from the oven and cut a slit into each ring to allow any steam to escape. Leave to cool.

In a mixing bowl whisk together the cream and Amaretto to stiff peaks. Cut the peaches or nectarines into thin slices, removing the stones. Spoon the cream into the second piping bag. Pipe a swirl of cream onto the buns. Top each with the fruit slices in pretty patterns and dust with icing sugar to serve. Store in the refrigerator if not serving straight away as they contain fresh cream. These are best eaten on the day they are made.

CHERRY CRUMBLE PARIS BRESTS

1 quantity Basic Choux
     Pastry (see page 8)

For the crumble mix
35 g self-raising flour
20 g butter
1 tablespoon caster sugar
icing sugar for dusting
     (optional)

For the filling
single quantity *crème
     pâtissière* (see page 9 but
     follow method here)
1 teaspoon almond extract
100 ml double cream
300 g cherry pie filling

a baking tray lined with baking
     parchment
2 piping bags, one fitted with
     a round and one with
     a star nozzle

Makes 12

These choux rings are topped with a crunchy buttery crumble mix and are filled with cherries and almond custard. They are utterly delicious! You can replace the cherries with different pie fillings if you wish to make other fruit crumble choux. Apple pie filling with vanilla custard works very well.

For the crumble topping place the flour, butter and caster sugar in a bowl and rub together with your fingertips to fine crumbs. Set aside until needed.

Preheat the oven to 200°C (400°F) Gas 6.

Spoon the choux pastry into one of the piping bags fitted with a round nozzle and pipe 12 rings of choux pastry onto the tray. Pat down any peaks in the pastry using a clean wet finger. Sprinkle over the crumble mix so that the top of each choux ring is covered lightly. Do not worry if any crumbles fall onto the tray. These can be discarded after baking (or eaten!). Sprinkle a little water into the bottom of the oven to create steam which will help the choux pastry to rise.

Bake in the oven for 10 minutes, then reduce the oven temperature to 180°C (350°F) Gas 4 and bake for a further 10–15 minutes until the pastry is crisp and the crumble mix is golden brown. Remove from the oven and cut a small slit into each pastry to allow steam to escape. Leave to cool.

Make the *crème pâtissière* following the instructions on page 9, adding the almond extract with the milk. Chill in the refrigerator until needed.

When you are ready to serve, whip the cream to stiff peaks then fold in the almond custard. Spoon into the other piping bag fitted with a star nozzle. Cut each bun in half and fill with custard and a spoonful of the cherry pie filling. Dust with icing sugar to serve, if desired. Serve straight away or store in the refrigerator. These buns are best eaten on the day they are made, although can be eaten the following day if stored in the refrigerator.

Chocolate and passion fruit are a super modern combination —
the tanginess of the fruit brings the chocolate to life.

PASSION FRUIT ÉCLAIRS

1 quantity Basic Choux
Pastry (see page 8)

For the mousse
200 g plain chocolate,
melted
3 passion fruit, skins
discarded
100 ml double cream
2 egg whites
20 g caster sugar

For the icing & decoration
180 g fondant icing
sugar, sifted
2–3 passion fruit, juiced
and seeds removed
50 g plain chocolate

a baking tray lined with
baking parchment
2 piping bags fitted with
large round nozzles

Makes 12

Begin by preparing the chocolate mousse as it needs time to set. Place the chocolate in a heatproof bowl set over a pan of simmering water until it is all melted. Stir the passion fruit juice, flesh and seeds, and double cream into the melted chocolate. The seeds of the passion fruit add a crunchy texture to these éclairs but if you are not keen on them, just remove them using a sieve and add the juice and flesh of the passion fruit to the chocolate mousse, leaving out the seeds. Whisk the egg whites to stiff peaks, then whisk in the caster sugar gradually. Fold the egg whites into the chocolate and leave to chill in the refrigerator for about 3 hours or overnight until the mousse is set.

Preheat the oven to 200°C (400°F) Gas 6.

Spoon the choux pastry into one of the piping bags and pipe 12 lines of pastry onto the baking tray about 10 cm in length, a small distance apart. Pat down any peaks in the pastry using a clean wet finger. Sprinkle a little water into the bottom of the oven to create steam which will help the choux pastry to rise.

Bake in the oven for 10 minutes, then reduce the oven temperature to 180°C (350°F) Gas 4 and bake for a further 15–20 minutes until the pastry is crisp. Remove from the oven and cut a small slit into each pastry to allow steam to escape. Leave to cool then cut the éclairs in half lengthways.

For the icing, mix the icing sugar with the passion fruit juice until you have a smooth icing, adding a little water if it is too stiff. This will depend on how much juice was released from your fruit so add gradually. Spread the icing over the tops of each éclair. Using a fork, drizzle thin lines of chocolate onto the icing and swirl in with a cocktail stick before the icing sets.

When you are ready to serve, spoon the choux pastry into the other piping bag and pipe a line of the chocolate passion fruit mousse into the bottom of each éclair. Cover with the iced tops and serve straight away or store in the refrigerator until needed. The éclairs are best eaten on the day they are made, although can be eaten the following day if you wish.

LEMON MERINGUE CHOUX BUNS

1 quantity Basic Choux
   Pastry (see page 8)

For the lemon filling
200 g white chocolate
125 ml double cream
2 tablespoon lemon curd
2 egg whites
2 tablespoon caster sugar

For the icing
160 g icing sugar, sifted
freshly squeezed juice
   of 1 lemon
yellow food colouring

For the meringue topping
100 g caster sugar
1 tablespoon golden syrup
60 ml water
2 egg whites

*a baking tray lined with
   baking parchment*
*3 piping bags, two fitted
   with round nozzles and
   one with a large star nozzle*
a chef's blow torch

Makes 14

Taking inspiration from the classic dessert lemon meringue pie, these dainty choux buns have a creamy lemon filling and are topped with a sharp lemon icing and fluffy meringue.

Begin by preparing the lemon mousse as it needs to set before being used to fill the choux buns. Melt the white chocolate in a heatproof bowl set over a saucepan of water, stirring occasionally. Once melted, remove from the heat and leave to cool slightly. Add the cream and lemon curd to the bowl and mix together to form a smooth paste. In a separate bowl, whisk the egg whites to stiff peaks. While still whisking, add the sugar gradually until the meringue is glossy. Gently fold the white chocolate mixture into the meringue. Leave in the refrigerator to set, for at least 3 hours or preferably overnight.

Preheat the oven to 200°C (400°F) Gas 6. Spoon the choux pastry into one of the piping bags fitted with a round nozzle and pipe 14 round balls onto the baking tray, a small distance apart. Pat down any peaks in the pastry using a clean wet finger. Sprinkle a little water into the bottom of the oven to create steam. Bake in the oven for 10 minutes, then reduce the oven temperature to 180°C (350°F) Gas 4 and bake for a further 15–20 minutes until the pastry is crisp. Remove from the oven and cut a small slit into each pastry to allow steam to escape. Leave to cool then make a small hole in the base of each bun.

For the icing, mix together the icing sugar with enough lemon juice until you have a smooth thick icing. Add a few drops of yellow food colouring if you wish. Dip the tops of the buns into the icing, invert and leave on a rack to set.

For the meringue, heat the sugar, syrup and water in a saucepan and bring to the boil. Whisk the egg whites to stiff peaks and then pour the hot syrup into the eggs, whisking all the time. It is best to do this with a stand mixer or if you do not have one, have someone else pour the hot syrup in while you whisk. Whisk for about 5 minutes until the meringue is stiff and glossy.

Place the lemon mousse into the other piping bag fitted with a round nozzle and pipe the mousse into each bun so that they are full. Spoon the meringue into the piping bag fitted with the star nozzle and pipe a large star of meringue on top of each bun. Using the blow torch, caramelize the meringue until lightly golden. The buns are best eaten on the day they are made.

These light choux buns are inspired by the popular dessert apple strudel; filled with fluffy apple scented with cinnamon and whipped cream.

STRUDEL CHOUX BUNS
with caramel glaze

2 quantity Basic Choux Pastry (see page 8)

For the baked apples
4 large cooking apples
120 g sultanas
1 teaspoon ground cinnamon
3 tablespoon golden syrup
60 ml water

For the caramel glaze
50 g caster sugar
1 tablespoon unsalted butter
a pinch of salt
60 ml double cream
180 g fondant icing sugar, sifted

To assemble
400 ml double cream, whipped to stiff peaks

an apple corer
2 baking trays lined with baking parchment
2 piping bags, one fitted with a large round nozzle and one with a large star nozzle

Makes 26

Preheat the oven to 180°C (350°F) Gas 4. Begin by preparing the apples as they need time to cool before being used to fill the choux buns. Core the apples and using a sharp knife cut a slit horizontally around the apples. Place the apples in an ovenproof dish. Mix the sultanas with the cinnamon and fill the core of each apple with them. Spoon some golden syrup over the filled core of each apple and add the water to the dish. Bake the apples for 40 minutes then turn the temperature down to 150°C (300°F) Gas 2 and cook for a further 30 minutes. Remove from the oven and leave to cool. Discard the skins and mix the apple, sultanas and syrup together.

Preheat the oven to 200°C (400°F) Gas 6. Spoon the choux pastry into the piping bag with a round nozzle and pipe 26 balls of pastry onto the baking trays, a small distance apart. Pat down any peaks in the pastry using a clean wet finger. Sprinkle a little water into the bottom of the oven to create steam. Bake each tray in the oven for 10 minutes, then reduce the oven temperature to 180°C (350°F) Gas 4 and bake for a further 15–20 minutes until the pastry is crisp. Remove from the oven and cut a small slit into each bun to allow the steam to escape. Leave to cool.

For the caramel glaze, place the sugar, butter and salt in a saucepan and simmer over a gentle heat until the sugar and butter have melted and the caramel is golden brown. Remove from the heat and allow to cool for a few minutes then pour in the cream and whisk together until the caramel is smooth and glossy. Strain to remove any crystallized sugar and leave to cool. Mix the icing sugar into the caramel sauce adding water if necessary then dip each bun into the glaze and leave on a rack to set.

When you are ready to serve, carefully cut each bun in half. Spoon the cream into the piping bag with a star nozzle and pipe a swirl of cream into the bottom of each bun. Top with a spoonful of the cooled apple. This will prevent the pastry becoming soggy from the apple. Top with the caramel glazed buns and serve straight away or store in the refrigerator until needed. The buns are best eaten on the day they are made.

FANCY

When raspberries are in season, these delicate choux rings are a perfect treat. With a rosy posy icing and crystallized rose petals, they make an elegant dessert bursting with tangy raspberries.

ROSE & RASPBERRY CHOUX RINGS

1 quantity Basic Choux Pastry (see page 8)

For the icing & decoration
150 g fondant icing sugar, sifted
1 tablespoon rose syrup
pink food colouring
crystallized rose petals

For the filling
300 ml double cream
1 tablespoon rose syrup
280 g raspberries

a large baking tray, lined with baking parchment or a silicon mat
2 piping bags, one fitted with a round and one with a star nozzle
10 paper cases, to serve

Makes 10

Preheat the oven to 200°C (400°F) Gas 6.

Spoon the choux pastry into the piping bag fitted with a round nozzle and pipe 10 rings of pastry, about 6 cm in diameter onto the baking tray, a small distance apart. Pat down any peaks in the pastry using a clean wet finger. Sprinkle a little water into the bottom of the oven to create steam which will help the choux pastry to rise.

Bake in the oven for 10 minutes, then reduce the oven temperature to 180°C (350°F) Gas 4 and bake for a further 15–20 minutes until the pastry is crisp. Remove from the oven and cut a small slit into each ring to allow any steam to escape and leave to cool. Carefully cut each ring in half horizontally using a sharp knife.

For the icing, mix the icing sugar with the rose syrup and a few drops of food colouring until you have a thick icing, adding a little water if needed. Spread a little icing over the tops of the choux rings. Decorate each top with some crystallized rose petals and then leave the icing to set.

Once the icing is set, whip the cream and rose syrup for the filling to stiff peaks then spoon into the piping bag fitted with a star nozzle. Pipe swirls of cream into the bottom of each ring. Top with fresh raspberries then place an iced ring on top of each one. Serve straight away or store in the refrigerator if you are not eating straight away. These choux buns are best eaten on the day they are made.

VIOLET ÉCLAIRS

1 quantity Basic Choux
    Pastry (see page 8)

For the icing
120 g fondant icing
    sugar, sifted
1 tablespoon violet syrup
    or liqueur
purple food colouring

For the filling
300 ml double cream
1 tablespoon violet syrup
    or liqueur

To decorate
crystallized violets

*a baking tray lined with baking
    parchment*
*2 piping bags one fitted with
    a large round nozzle and
    one with a star nozzle*

Makes 12

These éclairs are inspired by the childhood sweet Parma Violets which my Grandma used to buy me when I was little. The flavour comes from violet liqueur or violet syrup, both of which are available online or in good delicatessens. If violet flowers are in season you can crystallize them yourself following the instructions on page 49.

Preheat the oven to 200°C (400°F) Gas 6.

Spoon the choux pastry into the piping bag fitted with a round nozzle and pipe 12 lengths of pastry, about 10 cm long onto the baking tray, a small distance apart. Pat down any peaks in the pastry using a clean wet finger. Sprinkle a little water into the bottom of the oven to create steam which will help the choux pastry to rise.

Bake in the oven for 10 minutes, then reduce the oven temperature to 180°C (350°F) Gas 4 and bake for a further 15–20 minutes until the pastry is crisp. Remove from the oven and cut a small slit into each éclair with a sharp knife. Leave to cool.

Carefully cut each pastry in half horizontally using a sharp knife. For the icing, whisk together the icing sugar and violet syrup and a few drops of food colouring, if using, adding a few drops of water if necessary, and spread over the tops of the éclairs using a round-bladed knife. Decorate with the violets and leave to set.

For the filling, whisk together the cream and violet syrup (or liqueur) until the cream reaches stiff peaks. Spoon into the piping bag fitted with a star nozzle and carefully pipe a layer of cream into each éclair. Cover with the iced tops and serve straight away or store in the refrigerator until needed. The éclairs are best eaten on the day they are made, although can be eaten the following day if you wish.

Cooking with lavender from my garden is one of the things I like to do most. These profiteroles are served with a lavender syrup cream and are topped with a white chocolate sauce. Make sure that you use culinary lavender that has not been sprayed with any pesticides.

WHITE CHOCOLATE & LAVENDER PROFITEROLES

1 quantity Basic Choux Pastry (see page 8)

For the filling
80 g caster sugar
60 ml water
1 teaspoon culinary lavender buds
300 ml double cream

For the sauce & decoration
200 g cream-filled white chocolate (such as Lindor White) or white chocolate
200 ml double cream
1 tablespoon butter
purple edible glitter (optional)

2 baking trays lined with baking parchment
2 piping bags fitted with large round nozzles
a pestle and mortar
12–15 paper cases, to serve

Makes 25

Preheat the oven to 200°C (400°F) Gas 6. Spoon the choux pastry into one of the piping bags and pipe 25 small balls of choux pastry onto the trays. Pat down any peaks in the pastry using a clean wet finger. Sprinkle a little water into the bottom of the oven to create steam. Bake each tray in the oven for 10 minutes, then reduce the oven temperature to 180°C (350°F) Gas 4 and bake for a further 10–20 minutes until the pastry is crisp. Remove from the oven and cut a small slit into each with a sharp knife to let any steam escape. Leave to cool.

Place the sugar and water into a saucepan and simmer until the sugar has dissolved, then bring to the boil. Grind the lavender using a pestle and mortar and add to the sugar syrup. Simmer for a minute then remove from the heat and leave to cool completely. When you are ready to serve whisk the double cream and lavender syrup together to stiff peaks. Make a small hole in the bottom of each profiterole, using a sharp knife. Spoon the cream into a piping bag and pipe into the profiteroles.

For the sauce, place the chocolate in a heatproof bowl set over a saucepan of water and simmer until the chocolate is melted. Add the cream and the butter and stir until melted. Coat the profiteroles and sprinkle with edible glitter, or serve with the sauce on the side either warm or cold. The profiteroles are best eaten on the day they are made, although can be eaten the following day if stored in the refrigerator.

PISTACHIO RELIGIEUSE

1 quantity Basic Choux
  Pastry (see page 8)

For the filling & decoration
110 g shelled pistachios
  (unsalted)
30 g butter
20 g icing sugar, sifted
400 ml double cream

For the icing
150 g fondant icing sugar,
  sifted
green food colouring

*a baking tray lined with baking
  parchment*
*3 piping bags, two fitted with
  round nozzles and one
  with a small star nozzle*

Makes 12

Pistachios are an exotic nut with a perfumed flavour. Good quality pistachios have a vibrant green colour and when finely chopped make an elegant topping for these dainty *religieuse*.

Preheat the oven to 200°C (400°F) Gas 6.

Spoon the choux pastry into a piping bag fitted with a round nozzle and pipe 12 rings about 5 cm in diameter and 12 small balls of choux pastry onto the tray. Pat down any peaks in the pastry using a clean wet finger. Sprinkle a little water into the bottom of the oven to create steam which will help the choux pastry to rise.

Bake in the oven for 10 minutes, then reduce the oven temperature to 180°C (350°F) Gas 4 and bake for a further 15–20 minutes until the pastry is crisp. Remove from the oven and cut a small slit into each pastry to allow steam to escape. Leave to cool.

Reserve 12 whole pistachios for decoration, then blitz the remainder to very fine crumbs in a food processor or blender. Remove 3 tablespoons of the ground pistachios for decoration, then add the butter and icing sugar to the blender and blitz to a smooth paste to make pistachio butter. Whip the cream to stiff peaks. Remove a quarter of the cream and store in the fridge until you are ready to decorate. Make two small holes in the base of each ring, one on either side, and one small hole in each ball using a sharp knife. Fold the pistachio butter into the cream and spoon into a piping bag fitted with a round nozzle. Pipe the cream into each ring and ball, piping through both holes on the ring to make sure that they are generously filled.

For the icing, mix the icing sugar and food colouring with 1–2 tablespoons of cold water until you have a smooth thick icing. Spread some icing over each ring and sprinkle with the reserved chopped pistachios. Place one of the balls on top of each ring fixed in place with the icing and spread a little icing over the small balls. Place a whole pistachio on top. Spoon the reserved cream into the piping bag fitted with a small star nozzle and pipe small stars of cream onto the buns to decorate. Serve straight away or store in the refrigerator until needed. These buns are best eaten on the day they are made, although can be eaten the following day if you wish.

For a perfect afternoon tea why not serve these tea-infused buns topped with billowing sugar rose petals.

EARL GREY CHOUX BUNS

1 quantity Basic Choux
    Pastry (see page 8)

For the sugar rose petals
1 egg white
1 pesticide-free rose,
    separated into petals
caster sugar, for sprinkling

For the Earl Grey
crème pâtissière
60 ml boiling water
1 Earl Grey tea bag
1 quantity *créme pâtissière*
    (see page 9 but follow
    method here)

For the icing
150 g icing sugar, sifted
green food colouring

a clean small paint brush
a silicon mat
a large baking tray lined
    with baking parchment
    or a silicon mat
2 piping bags fitted with
    round nozzles
12 paper cases, to serve

Makes 12 buns

Begin by preparing the sugar rose petals as they need to dry overnight. Be careful to use roses which have not been sprayed with chemicals or pesticides. Whisk the egg white until it is foamy. Paint a thin layer of egg white on both the front and the back of a petal using the paint brush. Sprinkle it with caster sugar. This is best done by holding the caster sugar at a small height above the petal and sprinkling lightly. Have a plate below to catch any excess sugar. Repeat with all the remaining petals and place on a silicon mat in a warm place to dry overnight.

For the Earl Grey *crème pâtissière*, pour the boiling water over the teabag and leave to steep for a few minutes. Remove the teabag. Make the *crème pâtissière* following the instructions on page 9, adding the tea with the milk. Chill in the refrigerator until needed.

Preheat the oven to 200°C (400°F) Gas 6. Spoon the choux pastry into one of the piping bags and pipe 12 large balls of pastry onto the baking tray, a small distance apart. Pat down any peaks in the pastry using a clean wet finger. Sprinkle a little water into the bottom of the oven to create steam which will help the choux pastry to rise. Bake in the oven for 10 minutes, then reduce the oven temperature to 180°C (350°F) Gas 4 and bake for a further 15–20 minutes until the pastry is crisp. Remove from the oven and cut a small slit into each bun to allow any steam to escape. Leave to cool.

Make a small hole in the side of each bun with a sharp knife. Spoon the *crème pâtissière* into the other piping bag and fill each bun. Mix the icing to a stiff paste with a little water and add the food colouring. Spoon the icing on top of each bun and spread out using a round-bladed knife. Place a rose petal on top and fix with a little icing. Leave the icing to set and then serve straight away placed in paper cases. The buns are best eaten on the day they are made but can be stored in the refrigerator and eaten the following day if you wish.

HEART CHOUX BUNS

1 quantity Basic Choux
    Pastry (see page 8)

For the sugar glaze
180 g icing sugar, sifted
1 teaspoon vanilla extract
pink food colouring
sugar flowers, to decorate

For the marshmallow filling
200 g icing sugar, sifted
1 tablespoon butter,
    softened
3 tablespoons marshmallow
    fluff
1 tablespoon milk

2 baking trays lined with
    baking parchment
2 piping bags fitted with
    round nozzles

Makes 14

If you want to treat a loved one or are having a special
Valentine's or wedding tea, then these hearts are perfect
to serve. They are filled with a rich marshmallow frosting
and topped with a sugary pink glaze. There can be no better
way to say "I Love You".

Preheat the oven to 200°C (400°F) Gas 6.

Spoon the choux pastry into one of the piping bags and pipe 28 thin heart
shapes onto the baking trays. Do not pipe the hearts too thickly or they will lose
their heart shape as they bake. Pat down any peaks in the pastry using a clean wet
finger. Sprinkle a little water into the bottom of the oven to create steam which
will help the choux pastry to rise.

Bake in the oven for 10 minutes, then reduce the oven temperature to 180°C
(350°F) Gas 4 and bake for a further 5–10 minutes until the pastry is crisp. Remove
the hearts from the oven and cut a small slit into each pastry to allow steam to
escape. Leave to cool.

For the glaze, mix the icing sugar with 1–2 tablespoons of water, the vanilla
and a few drops of pink food colouring until you have a runny icing. Dip the
tops of 14 hearts into the icing, invert and place on a rack. It is best to have
a sheet of foil underneath to catch the icing drips. Decorate the iced hearts
with sugar flowers while the icing is still wet and leave to set completely.

For the marshmallow filling, whisk together the icing sugar, butter,
marshmallow fluff and milk until you have a smooth thick frosting. Spoon into
the other piping bag and pipe small blobs of icing onto the un-iced hearts
following the shape of the heart. Place a decorated heart on top of each to serve.
The hearts are best eaten on the day they are made, although can be eaten the
following day if you wish.

These quirky choux buns are filled with macadamia praline custard and are topped with a Matcha green tea icing.

MACADAMIA & MATCHA CHOUX BUNS

1 quantity Basic Choux
   Pastry (see page 8)

For the macadamia filling
& decoration
120 g caster sugar
150 g whole macadamia nuts
1 egg and 2 egg yolks
1 tablespoon cornflour
100 ml milk
350 ml double cream

For the icing
1 teaspoon Matcha green
   tea powder
150 g icing sugar, sifted
green food colouring

*a baking tray lined with baking
   parchment or a silicon mat*
*2 piping bags fitted with
   round nozzles*
*a silicon mat or greased
   baking tray*
18 wooden skewers
18 paper cases, to serve

Makes 18

Preheat the oven to 200°C (400°F) Gas 6. Spoon the choux pastry into one of the piping bags and pipe 18 small balls of choux pastry onto the baking trays. Pat down any peaks in the pastry using a clean wet finger. Sprinkle a little water into the bottom of the oven to create steam. Bake in the oven for 10 minutes, then reduce the oven temperature to 180°C (350°F) Gas 4 and bake for a further 15–20 minutes until the pastry is crisp. Remove from the oven and cut a small slit into each pastry with a sharp knife. Leave to cool then make a small hole in the bottom of each bun using a sharp knife.

For the macadamia custard and decorations, first heat 100 g caster sugar in a saucepan until it has melted. Leave to cool slightly until tacky then dip 18 individual nuts on wooden skewers into the caramel then hold upside down until set. Place the remaining nuts on the silicon mat or baking tray in a flat layer, then pour the liquid caramel over the nuts and leave to set. If your caramel has cooled down simply return the pan to the heat for a few minutes until runny. Once the layer of nuts has cooled, blitz in a blender to very fine praline crumbs. In a separate bowl, whisk the egg and egg yolks with the cornflour and 20 g caster sugar until very thick and pale yellow in colour. Place the milk and 150 ml of the cream in a saucepan and bring to the boil. Pour over the egg mixture, whisking all the time. Return to the pan and whisk over the heat until the mixture becomes very thick.

For the filling, whip the remaining cream to stiff peaks then fold in the macadamia custard and praline. Spoon into a piping bag and pipe the custard into each bun through the hole in the bottom of each bun.

For the icing, mix the Matcha powder with a tablespoon of hot water and make a paste. Add the Matcha paste to the icing sugar and mix together with a few drops of green food colouring and a little more water until you have a smooth thick icing. Cover each bun with icing, place a nut on top and leave to set. The buns are best eaten on the day they are made, as the caramelized nuts will become sticky over time when they are exposed to the air.

DESSERT

Filled with sweet Chantilly cream, ripe strawberries and strawberry jam with an extra crunch of almonds, this is a perfect summer's day dessert. If you prefer you can pipe small rings and make individual desserts.

STRAWBERRY CHOUX RING

2 quantities Basic Choux Pastry (see page 8)
25 g flaked almonds

To assemble
500 ml double cream
1 tablespoon icing sugar, sifted plus extra for dusting
1 teaspoon vanilla bean paste or vanilla extract
400 g ripe strawberries
2–3 tablespoon strawberry jam

a baking tray lined with baking parchment or a silicon mat
2 piping bags, one fitted with large round nozzle and one with a large star nozzle

Serves 8

Preheat the oven to 200°C (400°F) Gas 6.

Spoon the choux pastry into the piping bag fitted with a round nozzle and pipe large balls of the paste in a ring about 22 cm in diameter on the lined baking tray. Pat down any peaks in the pastry using a clean wet finger. Sprinkle the top of the ring with the flaked almonds. Then sprinkle a little water into the bottom of the oven to create steam which will help the choux pastry to rise.

Bake in the oven for 20 minutes, then reduce the oven temperature to 180°C (350°F) Gas 4 and bake for a further 25 minutes until the pastry is crisp. Remove from the oven and cut a few slits into the ring using a sharp knife to allow any steam to escape, then return to the oven for a further 5 minutes. Remove from the oven and leave to cool.

Once cool, cut the ring in half horizontally using a large serrated knife. The ring is fragile so you need to cut carefully. Do not worry too much if the top of the ring breaks as you can sandwich it back together with the cream filling.

Place the cream, icing sugar and vanilla bean paste in a mixing bowl and whisk to stiff peaks. Spoon the cream into the piping bag fitted with the star nozzle and pipe swirls of cream onto the bottom of each choux ball in the ring around the outside edge, reserving a little cream to decorate the top.

Reserve a few strawberries for decoration, then hull the remaining strawberries and cut into halves. Place the halved strawberries on top of the cream and top with small teaspoons of strawberry jam. Carefully lift and place the almond-topped choux ring on top of the cream and strawberries. Dust with icing sugar and then pipe small stars of cream on top of the ring before carefully placing the reserved strawberries on top.

Serve straight away or store in the refrigerator until needed. This is best eaten on the day it is made, although can be eaten the following day if you wish.

CARAMEL ALMOND PROFITEROLES

1 quantity Basic Choux
   Pastry (see page 8)
20 g flaked almonds

For the filling
1 heaped tablespoon
   almond butter
250 ml double cream

For the sauce
100 g caster sugar
50 g butter
1 tablespoon Amaretto
   or almond liqueur
80 ml double cream

2 baking trays lined with
   baking parchment
   or silicon mats
2 piping bags fitted with
   large round nozzles

Makes 25

These caramel profiteroles are topped with crunchy almonds and filled with an almond cream, made with almond butter. If you are not able to find almond butter then you can make your own at home using the method below.

Preheat the oven to 200°C (400°F) Gas 6. Spoon the choux pastry into one of the piping bags and pipe 25 small balls of dough onto the baking trays, a small distance apart. Pat down any peaks in the pastry using a clean wet finger. Sprinkle the almonds over the top of the buns, then sprinkle a little water into the bottom of the oven to create steam which will help the choux pastry to rise. Bake each tray in the oven for 10 minutes, then reduce the oven temperature to 180°C (350°F) Gas 4 and bake for a further 15–20 minutes until the pastry is crisp. Remove from the oven and cut a small slit into each bun with a sharp knife to allow any steam to escape. Leave to cool.

Place the almond butter in a bowl with the cream and whisk to stiff peaks. Make a hole in the bottom of each bun with a sharp knife. Spoon the cream into the other piping bag and pipe into each bun until they are full.

If you are not able to find almond butter, place 100 g roasted skinned almonds in a blender with a tablespoon of icing sugar and blitz until they become a sticky paste. You may need to stop and scrape the nuts down from the sides of the blender part way through blending. Leave the paste to cool, as it will become hot during blending, before using.

For the sauce, heat the sugar and butter in a saucepan until the sugar and butter have melted and start to caramelize. Cook over the heat until the caramel starts to turn light golden brown, add the Amaretto to the pan and simmer for a further few minutes. Add the cream to the pan, stir and remove from the heat.

Serve the buns straight away with the warm caramel sauce.

The profiteroles are best eaten on the day they are made, although can be eaten the following day if stored in the refrigerator.

For a party or great after dinner dessert, why not serve these peppermint profiteroles filled with cold ice cream and topped with warm chocolate mint sauce. Garnished with mint leaves, these buns make the perfect end to any meal. If you wish you can crystallize the mint leaves following the instructions on page 49 for a pretty effect.

AFTER DINNER PROFITEROLES

1 quantity Basic Choux Pastry (see page 8)

For the chocolate mint sauce
180 g chocolate fondant-filled mints (such as After Eight)
125 ml double cream

For the filling
300 g mint choc chip ice cream or other flavour of your choosing

To decorate
mint leaves

a baking tray lined with baking parchment
2 piping bags fitted with large round nozzles

Makes 16

Preheat the oven to 200°C (400°F) Gas 6. Spoon the choux pastry into one of the piping bags and pipe 16 balls of pastry onto the baking tray, a small distance apart. Pat down any peaks in the pastry using a clean wet finger. Sprinkle a little water into the bottom of the oven. This will create steam which will help the choux pastry to rise. Bake in the oven for 10 minutes, then reduce the oven temperature to 180°C (350°F) Gas 4 and bake for a further 15–20 minutes until the pastry is crisp. Remove from the oven and cut a small slit into each bun to allow any steam to escape. Leave to cool. Cut a small hole into the bottom of each bun with a sharp knife, ready for piping later.

For the chocolate mint sauce, place the chocolate mints and cream in a saucepan and simmer over a gentle heat until the mints have melted and the sauce is glossy.

Bring the ice cream to room temperature so that it is soft enough to pipe. Spoon into the other piping bag and working quickly pipe the ice cream into the buns. Serve straight away with the hot mint sauce and decorate with mint leaves. Alternatively you can freeze the filled buns for up to one month and defrost them slightly before serving, making the sauce at the time you wish to serve the profiteroles.

"*Croque en bouche*" after which this spectacular dessert is named literally translates as "crunch in the mouth" referring to the crack of the sugar coating when you bite into the profiteroles. This recipe creates a 40-cm tower but *croquembouche* can be made smaller (as photographed opposite).

CROQUEMBOUCHE

4 quantities Basic Choux Pastry (see page 8)

For the filling
3 quantities mousse (see page 35 and exclude the passion fruit)

To assemble
800 g caster sugar
sugar nibs and rice paper or sugar flowers, to decorate (optional)

4 baking trays lined with baking parchment or silicon mats (or rewash and dry between use)
2 piping bags filled with round nozzles
a large sheet of thin cardboard

Makes 80 profiteroles
to serve 20–30 people

Begin by preparing the chocolate mousse as it needs time to set (see page 35).

Preheat the oven to 200°C (400°F) Gas 6. Spoon the choux pastry into one of the piping bags and pipe about 80 small balls of pastry onto the trays, a small distance apart. Using a clean wet finger smooth down any peaks. Sprinkle a little water into the bottom of the oven to create steam which will help the choux pastry to rise. Bake each tray in the oven for 10 minutes, then reduce the oven temperature to 180°C (350°F) Gas 4 and bake for a further 10–15 minutes until the pastry is crisp. Remove from the oven and cut a slit into each profiterole to allow any steam to escape. Leave to cool. Repeat with the remaining trays until all the profiteroles are cooked. Once cooled, make a small hole in the base of each bun using a sharp knife.

Spoon the mousse into the other piping bag and pipe the chocolate mousse into each profiterole until they are full. Make a cone with the cardboard which is approximately 40 cm in height and 18 cm in diameter across the base, securing in place with adhesive tape. Place the cone in the centre of a large plate or cake stand.

In a saucepan, heat the caster sugar until melted. It is best to do this in two saucepans, heating half the sugar in each. Do not stir the pan as the sugar is cooking but swirl it to ensure that the sugar does not burn. Once melted, carefully dip each bun into the caramel using tongs or your fingers but take extreme care as the sugar is very hot. Coat the profiteroles one at a time and place in a ring around the base of the cone. Repeat with all the remaining profiteroles, layer by layer, until the whole cone is covered. If you wish, dip the caramel coated profiteroles in sugar nibs for decoration. You need to work quickly before the sugar sets. If the sugar sets too quickly, just return it to the heat for a few minutes to melt it again. Once the whole tower is assembled, dip a fork into the remaining sugar and then spin it over the tower of profiteroles in thin lines to make spun sugar. Attach rice paper or sugar flowers using a little of the sugar and serve straight away as the spun sugar will deteriorate and become sticky when exposed to the air.

This is a spectacular dessert for a special occasion, filled with roasted cinnamon plums and custard and topped with sugar-coated profiteroles.

GÂTEAU ST HONORÉ

2 quantities Basic Choux
Pastry (see page 8)

For the roasted plums
400 g plums, halved and
stoned
2 teaspoons ground
cinnamon
1 tablespoon caster sugar

For the filling
300 ml cream
1 tablespoon icing
sugar, sifted
seeds of 1 vanilla pod

For the gateaux base
plain flour, for dusting
500 g puff pastry

For the caramel
& decoration
200 g caster sugar

2 baking trays lined
with baking parchment
or silicon mats
an ovenproof roasting dish
3 piping bags, two fitted with
round nozzles and one
with a star nozzle

Serves 12

Preheat the oven to 180°C (350°F) Gas 4. Place the plums, cinnamon and sugar in an ovenproof dish with a tablespoon or two of water and bake for about 20 minutes until the plums are just soft. Leave to cool.

For a second time, preheat the oven to 200°C (400°F) Gas 6. On a flour-dusted surface, roll out the puff pastry thinly, then cut out a large circle about 28 cm in diameter. This is easiest done by cutting round a dinner plate. Prick the top of the pastry all over with a fork. Spoon the choux pastry into a piping bag fitted with a round nozzle and pipe a line of choux around the edge of the puff pastry and then a spiral in the centre. Pipe the remaining choux into small round balls onto the other baking tray. Pat down any peaks in the pastry using a clean wet finger. Bake the puff pastry in the oven for 15 minutes, then reduce the oven temperature to 180°C and bake for a further 20–30 minutes until the pastry is crisp and golden brown. Repeat with the choux buns, baking for 10 minutes at 200°C, then for a further 15–20 minutes at 180°C until the pastry is crisp. Remove from the oven and cut a slit into the choux buns using a sharp knife. Leave to cool.

For the filling, whip the cream with the icing sugar and vanilla seeds to stiff peaks, place into the piping bag fitted with a round nozzle and fill each bun, reserving some cream for decoration. For the caramel, heat the caster sugar in a heavy-based saucepan. Do not stir the sugar but swirl the pan to prevent the sugar from burning. The sugar will start to caramelize. Once the caramel is a golden colour, remove from the heat. Using kitchen tongs dip the top of each choux bun into the caramel and then place in a ring around the edge of the puff pastry, fixing in place with a little cream and extra caramel if needed. If the caramel starts to set, return the pan to the heat for a further minute or so until it melts again.

Once the profiterole ring is in place, fill the centre cavity with custard, top with the roasted plums and then pipe the cream on top. To prepare the spun sugar decoration, reheat the caramel for a few minutes until the caramel is liquid. Leave to cool slightly then dip a fork into the sugar and pull it away from the pan to make long fine caramel strands. The spun sugar will melt when exposed to the air for a period of time so this needs to be served within a few hours of being decorated.

INDEX